2017 SQA Past Papers with Answers

National 5
GERMAN

FREE
audio files to accompany this title can
be accessed at
**www.hoddereducation.co.uk/
sqaaudiofiles**
You will find the files listed
by language and level.

2015, 2016 & 2017 Exams

Hodder Gibson Study Skills Advice – National 5 German — – page 3
Hodder Gibson Study Skills Advice – General — – page 5
2015 EXAM — – page 9
2016 EXAM — – page 39
2017 EXAM — – page 69
ANSWERS — – page 101

**HODDER
GIBSON**
AN HACHETTE UK COMPANY

This book contains the official SQA 2015, 2016 and 2017 Exams for National 5 German, with associated SQA-approved answers modified from the official marking instructions that accompany the paper.

In addition the book contains study skills advice. This advice has been specially commissioned by Hodder Gibson, and has been written by experienced senior teachers and examiners in line with the new National 5 syllabus and assessment outlines. This is not SQA material but has been devised to provide further guidance for National 5 examinations.

Hodder Gibson is grateful to the copyright holders, as credited on the final page of the Answer section, for permission to use their material. Every effort has been made to trace the copyright holders and to obtain their permission for the use of copyright material. Hodder Gibson will be happy to receive information allowing us to rectify any error or omission in future editions.

Hachette UK's policy is to use papers that are natural, renewable and recyclable products and made from wood grown in sustainable forests. The logging and manufacturing processes are expected to conform to the environmental regulations of the country of origin.

Orders: please contact Bookpoint Ltd, 130 Park Drive, Milton Park, Abingdon, Oxon OX14 4SE. Telephone: (44) 01235 827720. Fax: (44) 01235 400454. Lines are open 9.00–5.00, Monday to Saturday, with a 24-hour message answering service. Visit our website at www.hoddereducation.co.uk. Hodder Gibson can be contacted direct on: Tel: 0141 333 4650; Fax: 0141 404 8188; email: hoddergibson@hodder.co.uk

This collection first published in 2017 by
Hodder Gibson, an imprint of Hodder Education,
An Hachette UK Company
211 St Vincent Street
Glasgow G2 5QY

Typeset by Aptara, Inc.

Printed in the UK

A catalogue record for this title is available from the British Library

ISBN: 978-1-5104-2190-5

2 1

2018 2017

MIX
Paper from
responsible sources
FSC™ C104740

Introduction

National 5 German

You have chosen to add a national qualification in German to your education. Congratulations – it is one of the most sought-after foreign languages for business and trade in Scotland and in Europe.

What can National 5 do for you?

National 5 German is a course which has been developed by teachers and educational leaders to meet the requirements for Modern Foreign Languages in the 21st century.

The aim of the course is to give you confidence in understanding (reading and listening) and using (talking and writing) German in the following contexts:

- Society (Family and friends, Lifestyle, Media, Global languages, Citizenship)
- Learning (Learning in context, Education)
- Employability (Jobs, Work and CVs)
- Culture (Planning a trip, Other countries, Celebrating a special event, German literature, German films and TV)

What does the Course Assessment look like?

Reading and Writing

You will have 1 hour and 30 minutes for both parts of this paper. This question paper will have 50 marks in total – 37.5% of the overall course marks.

The Reading paper

The reading part of this paper will have 30 marks – 10 marks for each text.

You will read three German texts of between 150 and 200 words each. Questions on the text are set in English, and you must respond in English. These questions will ask for specific details about the text.

You may use a dictionary in this paper.

The Writing paper

You will produce one written text, a job application in German, in response to a stimulus supported by six bullet points which you must address. See them as a checklist of information that you will have to provide in your response.

Four of the bullet points are predictable but two of them are less predictable as they vary from year to year.

The text you produce must take the form of an e-mail and should be between 120 to 150 words in length.

You may use a dictionary in this paper.

You will also have to produce an essay in class which will be sent away to be marked by the SQA.

You can write about anything you want or your teacher may provide you with a topic to write about.

You should write 120–200 words in German and it must be your own work.

You can use your jotters, a dictionary or a word list to help you, but you are not allowed to use textbooks or vocabulary sheets with sentences on it.

Your teacher is allowed to correct your work using a correction code, which you can use to help you redraft.

Your final draft will make up half of your writing mark.

Listening

The Listening paper

This question paper will have 20 marks – 25% of the total mark.

You will listen to one monologue (approximately one and a half minutes long) and one short dialogue (approximately two to two and a half minutes long) in German. You will be asked questions in English and must respond in English.

The monologue is worth 8 marks and the dialogue is worth 12 marks. The dialogue will be linked to the context to the monologue.

You may not use a dictionary in this paper.

Talking

The talking assessment will be carried out in your school by your German teacher, who will be able to help you to prepare for it well in advance. It will be recorded and marked by your teacher.

The talking assessment has two parts:

1 **A presentation in German on a topic of your choice**, such as:
- Meine Familie und ich
- Meine Freizeit und meine Freunde
- Meine Heimatstadt
- Meine Schule und meine Schulkarriere
- Meine Zukunftspläne
- Mein Arbeitspraktikum
- Mein Lieblingsfilm
- Mein Lieblingsbuch

The presentation should be approximately one to two minutes long, you may use notes (not sentences) and/or visual support such as a PowerPoint presentation, a picture, a photograph, an item, etc.

2 A discussion with your teacher in German

Your teacher will ask you additional questions on your presentation or may ask questions which relate to a topic derived from your presentation. The discussion should be approximately three to five minutes long.

The total mark for your Talking exam at National 5 is 30. Five out of these 30 marks will only be granted if the language you use in the conversation is natural and spontaneous.

What can you do to help you have a successful National 5 German exam?

Top Tip: Do not panic!

As soon as the exam timetable is published, ask your teacher for the exact date of the German exam (usually April/May time) and mark the date and time in your diary – or on your mobile phone.

Remember that your Talking exam will be done before your Reading and Writing and Listening exams. Take this into account when you plan your revision.

Reading tips

Before you read the German texts:

- read the title/headline and ask yourself what you already know about the topic.
- look at any pictures as they support the contents of a text.
- check if the text comes with a glossary to save yourself time looking up words in the dictionary.

While you are reading the German texts:

- focus on your reading – be an active reader!
- try to figure out the main idea(s) of the text(s).
- access the meaning of a word by
  - checking the context/sentence the word is in.
  - checking if the word is similar to English (German and English have many cognates or near cognates – which are words that look and/ or sound similar or even the same); many German and English words begin with the same letter or even the same two letters.
  - checking whether or not the text comes with a glossary.
  - using the dictionary.

After you have read the text and before you start answering the questions:

- read the comprehension questions carefully.
- if necessary, underline the question word to highlight exactly what kind of answer is required.
- check the tense form of the English question to make sure you use the same tense form in your answer.
- make sure that your answer has sufficient detail – compare it with the marks you can get for each answer.

Most importantly – make sure your English answers make sense and your English expression is of a good standard.

After you have answered the questions:

- allow yourself time to go over your answers.

Writing tips

Before you sit your Writing exam:

- plan the exam carefully by exploring the four predictable bullet points:
  - Make sure you know the proper conventions for your piece of writing and practise them.
  - Make a note of some vocabulary which you will need to address these bullet points and learn it. Choose five verbs, five adjectives and five nouns, for example.
  - Remember what you have practised in class when covering the topic areas you are writing about.
  - Produce a draft and show it to your teacher before the exam.

While you are sitting your Writing exam:

- read the stimulus very carefully and identify exactly what the job is that you are going to apply for. Use the dictionary for help, if necessary, and remember that jobs in German have male and female forms.
- read the two bullet points which are less predictable. Remember what you have learned in class about the topics they address.
- avoid writing very long sentences as you may lose control of structure and word order. However, try to include connectors such as und/aber/oder/denn and also some which change the word order such as weil/obwohl/dass.
- try to use different tense forms where possible, e.g. „Ich habe im letzten Jahr ein Arbeitspraktikum gemacht."/ „Ich werde das Abitur machen und Deutsch studieren."

- where possible, include opinions using German expressions such as „Ich denke, dass..."/ „Ich bin der Meinung, dass..."/ „Ich finde..."/ „Meiner Meinung nach..."
- try not to translate from English as you will be tempted to apply the English sentence structure rather than the German one – focus on the correct position of the verb in the German sentence and remember the rules of German sentence structure.
- limit yourself to 20 to 25 words per bullet point and make sure you address them all.
- focus on capitalisation of nouns and correct verb endings to achieve a high level of accuracy.

After you have finished your Writing exam:

- leave yourself enough time at the end to proofread your e-mail text.
- check that you have addressed all six bullet points.
- check your verb endings and tense forms, your adjective endings and capitalisation of nouns.
- if in doubt, use the dictionary for support.

Listening tips

Top tip: Learn your vocabulary regularly and revise systematically before the exam. Only those who recognise words will be able to understand the meaning of a spoken sentence.

Before you sit your Listening exam:

- revise vocabulary, especially verbs in their different tense forms, quantifiers (viel, wenig, die meisten), numbers and dates. Read vocabulary out loud so that you recognise acoustically what you see in front of you.
- read the title/the introduction to the listening item and ask yourself what your experience with the topic is and what you know about this topic.
- remember the close relationship between the English and the German language where many words sound very similar and use this to your benefit in listening. However, beware: "Schinken" is not "chicken"!
- read the English questions very carefully – you have one minute to study them – and underline the question words or any others which you feel might be of importance.
- remember that the questions are in chronological sequence – the answer to question (c) must be between the answers to (b) and (d) in the recording.

While you are sitting your Listening exam:

- remember that both items (monologue and dialogue) will be played three times so it is not necessary to answer any questions during the first playing.
- write your answers neatly and clearly on your question paper. If you correct your answer, make sure the marker will be able to recognise your final answer.
- if you don't understand a word which you believe to be an element of an answer – do not panic! Trust your instincts and your natural connection to German as a speaker of English and see if you can guess the meaning.
- be guided by the number of marks allocated to each question. They will tell you how much information is expected in your answer.

After your Listening exam:

- go over your answers. Make sure your English expression is as good as possible to convey meaning clearly.
- make sure you have crossed out any draft answers leaving the final answer for the marker to see.

Talking tips

Top tips:

- **Start preparing for your Talking exam in plenty of time. Practise talking regularly as practice makes perfect.**
- **Remember that your teacher will conduct the exam and that he/she will want to help you to succeed. Trust him/her.**

Before your Talking exam:

- choose a topic that you really like and have something to say about for your presentation.
- develop a piece of writing for your presentation which has a clear structure. Show this work to your teacher.
- ask your teacher to read aloud and record this text for you on your mobile phone, iPod or any other media device so that you can listen to it many times before the exam.
- turn the sentences of that text into notes. (A note is a short phrase which does not contain a verb.)
- practise your presentation by listening to the recording and reading your notes, then try it without the recording by your teacher.
- try to figure out what kind of questions your teacher might ask you in the discussion. These questions will be linked to the topic you have presented.

For example:

If you have done a presentation on your favourite film, your teacher might ask questions such as:

- „Siehst du gern fern oder gehst du lieber ins Kino?"
- „Was findest du besser – DVDs zu Hause oder einen Kinofilm mit Freunden?"
- „Hast du einen Lieblingsschauspieler/eine Lieblingsschauspielerin? Warum findest du ihn/sie gut?"
- „Welche Filme siehst du gern?"
- „Welche Fernsehsendungen siehst du gern?"

Make sure you revise and learn conventions on expressing an opinion in German, e.g. „Ich finde ...", „Ich bin der Meinung, dass...", „Meiner Meinung nach..." etc.

You should also revise and learn conventions on how to sustain a conversation – especially when you have difficulties understanding a question, e.g. „Ich habe das nicht verstanden. Bitte wiederholen Sie die Frage."/ „Ich bin nicht sicher, was das auf Deutsch/Englisch heißt."/ „Sprechen Sie bitte langsamer."

During your Talking exam:

- concentrate on your notes in your presentation. You are entitled to use them – do not do without.
- look up from your notes, keep eye contact and speak loudly and clearly to show you are confident – and to ensure a good quality of recording!
- do not panic if you are stuck – try to recover by remembering what you have worked out for your presentation.
- listen carefully to your teacher's questions and remember that you can always "steal" vocabulary from the question to make your answer.
- try to avoid very long sentences as you might lose control over the sentence structure. However, try to use connectors such as und/aber/oder/denn and also weil.
- ask for help (in German) when you need it. This will not necessarily result in a lower mark as it shows your ability to use German for clarification purposes.

After your Talking exam:

- ask your teacher if it is possible to listen to your recording and get some feedback on your performance.
- you might want to use your National 5 Talking exam as a basis for your Higher Talking exam – so keep your notes if you are thinking about taking Higher German.

In your National 5 Course Assessment, the formula to success is a sound knowledge of the level of German required, teamwork in class and with your teacher, and confidence in yourself and the skills your teacher has helped you to develop. Most importantly though, enjoy the course and the experience. Deutsch ist mega cool!

Good luck!

Remember that the rewards for passing National 5 German are well worth it! Your pass will help you get the future you want for yourself. In the exam, be confident in your own ability. If you're not sure how to answer a question, trust your instincts and just give it a go anyway. Keep calm and don't panic! GOOD LUCK!

Study Skills – what you need to know to pass exams!

Pause for thought

Many students might skip quickly through a page like this. After all, we all know how to revise. Do you really though?

Think about this:

"IF YOU ALWAYS DO WHAT YOU ALWAYS DO, YOU WILL ALWAYS GET WHAT YOU HAVE ALWAYS GOT."

Do you like the grades you get? Do you want to do better? If you get full marks in your assessment, then that's great! Change nothing! This section is just to help you get that little bit better than you already are.

There are two main parts to the advice on offer here. The first part highlights fairly obvious things but which are also very important. The second part makes suggestions about revision that you might not have thought about but which WILL help you.

Part 1

DOH! It's so obvious but …

Start revising in good time

Don't leave it until the last minute – this will make you panic.

Make a revision timetable that sets out work time AND play time.

Sleep and eat!

Obvious really, and very helpful. Avoid arguments or stressful things too – even games that wind you up. You need to be fit, awake and focused!

Know your place!

Make sure you know exactly **WHEN and WHERE** your exams are.

Know your enemy!

Make sure you know what to expect in the exam.

How is the paper structured?

How much time is there for each question?

What types of question are involved?

Which topics seem to come up time and time again?

Which topics are your strongest and which are your weakest?

Are all topics compulsory or are there choices?

Learn by DOING!

There is no substitute for past papers and practice papers – they are simply essential! Tackling this collection of papers and answers is exactly the right thing to be doing as your exams approach.

Part 2

People learn in different ways. Some like low light, some bright. Some like early morning, some like evening / night. Some prefer warm, some prefer cold. But everyone uses their BRAIN and the brain works when it is active. Passive learning – sitting gazing at notes – is the most INEFFICIENT way to learn anything. Below you will find tips and ideas for making your revision more effective and maybe even more enjoyable. What follows gets your brain active, and active learning works!

Activity 1 – Stop and review

Step 1

When you have done no more than 5 minutes of revision reading STOP!

Step 2

Write a heading in your own words which sums up the topic you have been revising.

Step 3

Write a summary of what you have revised in no more than two sentences. Don't fool yourself by saying, "I know it, but I cannot put it into words". That just means you don't know it well enough. If you cannot write your summary, revise that section again, knowing that you must write a summary at the end of it. Many of you will have notebooks full of blue/black ink writing. Many of the pages will not be especially attractive or memorable so try to liven them up a bit with colour as you are reviewing and rewriting. **This is a great memory aid, and memory is the most important thing.**

Activity 2 – Use technology!

Why should everything be written down? Have you thought about "mental" maps, diagrams, cartoons and colour to help you learn? And rather than write down notes, why not record your revision material?

What about having a text message revision session with friends? Keep in touch with them to find out how and what they are revising and share ideas and questions.

Why not make a video diary where you tell the camera what you are doing, what you think you have learned and what you still have to do? No one has to see or hear it, but the process of having to organise your thoughts in a formal way to explain something is a very important learning practice.

Be sure to make use of electronic files. You could begin to summarise your class notes. Your typing might be slow, but it will get faster and the typed notes will be easier to read than the scribbles in your class notes. Try to add different fonts and colours to make your work stand out. You can easily Google relevant pictures, cartoons and diagrams which you can copy and paste to make your work more attractive and **MEMORABLE**.

Activity 3 – This is it. Do this and you will know lots!

Step 1

In this task you must be very honest with yourself! Find the SQA syllabus for your subject (www.sqa.org.uk). Look at how it is broken down into main topics called MANDATORY knowledge. That means stuff you MUST know.

Step 2

BEFORE you do ANY revision on this topic, write a list of everything that you already know about the subject. It might be quite a long list but you only need to write it once. It shows you all the information that is already in your long-term memory so you know what parts you do not need to revise!

Step 3

Pick a chapter or section from your book or revision notes. Choose a fairly large section or a whole chapter to get the most out of this activity.

With a buddy, use Skype, Facetime, Twitter or any other communication you have, to play the game "If this is the answer, what is the question?". For example, if you are revising Geography and the answer you provide is "meander", your buddy would have to make up a question like "What is the word that describes a feature of a river where it flows slowly and bends often from side to side?".

Make up 10 "answers" based on the content of the chapter or section you are using. Give this to your buddy to solve while you solve theirs.

Step 4

Construct a wordsearch of at least 10 × 10 squares. You can make it as big as you like but keep it realistic. Work together with a group of friends. Many apps allow you to make wordsearch puzzles online. The words and phrases can go in any direction and phrases can be split. Your puzzle must only contain facts linked to the topic you are revising. Your task is to find 10 bits of information to hide in your puzzle, but you must not repeat information that you used in Step 3. DO NOT show where the words are. Fill up empty squares with random letters. Remember to keep a note of where your answers are hidden but do not show your friends. When you have a complete puzzle, exchange it with a friend to solve each other's puzzle.

Step 5

Now make up 10 questions (not "answers" this time) based on the same chapter used in the previous two tasks. Again, you must find NEW information that you have not yet used. Now it's getting hard to find that new information! Again, give your questions to a friend to answer.

Step 6

As you have been doing the puzzles, your brain has been actively searching for new information. Now write a NEW LIST that contains only the new information you have discovered when doing the puzzles. Your new list is the one to look at repeatedly for short bursts over the next few days. Try to remember more and more of it without looking at it. After a few days, you should be able to add words from your second list to your first list as you increase the information in your long-term memory.

FINALLY! Be inspired...

Make a list of different revision ideas and beside each one write **THINGS I HAVE** tried, **THINGS I WILL** try and **THINGS I MIGHT** try. Don't be scared of trying something new.

And remember – "FAIL TO PREPARE AND PREPARE TO FAIL!"

NATIONAL 5

2015

National
Qualifications
2015

Mark 23/30 77%

X734/75/01

German Reading

TUESDAY, 26 MAY
9:00 AM – 10:30 AM

Fill in these boxes and read what is printed below.

Full name of centre

Town

Forename(s)

Surname

Number of seat

Date of birth
Day   Month   Year   Scottish candidate number

Total marks — 30

Attempt ALL questions.

Write your answers clearly, in **English**, in the spaces provided in this booklet.

You may use a German dictionary.

Additional space for answers is provided at the end of this booklet. If you use this space you must clearly identify the question number you are attempting.

Use **blue** or **black** ink.

There is a separate question and answer booklet for Writing. You must complete your answer for Writing in the question and answer booklet for Writing.

Before leaving the examination room you must give both booklets to the Invigilator; if you do not, you may lose all the marks for this paper.

MARKS | DO NOT WRITE IN THIS MARGIN

Total marks — 30

Attempt ALL questions

Text 1

This passage is about exam stress and how to overcome this.

Prüfungsangst — dieses Gefühl, das jeder kennt. Viele Leute zittern, wenn sie das Wort „Prüfung" hören.

Wenn man sich auf eine Prüfung gut vorbereiten will, sollte man die Zeit gut planen. Man sollte zum Beispiel nicht stundenlang am Schreibtisch sitzen — eine kleine Pause alle neunzig Minuten ist die beste Belohnung.

Laura, 16, ist Schülerin am Schiller-Gymnasium in Hamburg: „Vor einer Prüfung habe ich meistens schwitzige Hände und habe keinen Appetit mehr. Wenn ich etwas lernen muss, schreibe ich eine Frage auf eine Karte und auf die Rückseite kommt dann die Antwort. Wenn ich eine mündliche Prüfung habe, übe ich mit einer Freundin. Das machen wir in einer neuen Umgebung, vielleicht in einem Café in der Stadt oder in der Schulbibliothek."

Lars Ritter ist Direktor der Rhein-Schule in Köln und er kennt die Sorgen, die Schüler in der Prüfungszeit erleben: „Wir sagen den Schülern, dass Prüfungsangst normal und sogar nötig ist. Ohne Angst würde man die Prüfungssituation nicht ernst nehmen. Negative Gedanken so wie: ‚Durchfallen wäre eine Katastrophe', muss man vergessen. Viel besser ist es, wenn man denkt: ‚Ich habe mich auf die Prüfung vorbereitet und ich hoffe, dass ich eine gute Note bekomme.'"

Questions

(a) How do many people react to the mention of exams? Complete the following sentence.   ①

Lots of people ___Shudder___ when they hear the word "exam".

(b) What is the best way to plan your time for studying? Give **two** details.   ②

___don't sit for hours at a desk and take a break___

___every 90 minutes___

MARKS | DO NOT WRITE IN THIS MARGIN

Text 1 Questions (continued)

(c) How does Laura react before exams? State any **one** thing.

She hasn't got an apetite

1

(d) (i) How does she prepare for **speaking** exams?

She pratices with her friends

1

  (ii) Where does she do this? State any **one** thing.

in a Café in the city

1

(e) What does headmaster Lars Ritter say to his pupils about exam nerves? State **two** things.

That it's normal and even necessary

2 | 1

(f) Lars Ritter gives examples of the negative and positive thoughts students can have about exams.

  (i) Which negative thought does he mention?

Failing would be a catastrophe

1

  (ii) Give **one** of the positive thoughts students might have.

I have prepared for the exam and I hope to get good marks

1

[Turn over

MARKS

DO NOT WRITE IN THIS MARGIN

Text 2

Lisa Wiedermann recently visited India and spent time at an international school.

Im Februar dieses Jahres hatte ich die Gelegenheit, mit einer Gruppe nach Indien zu fahren. Die Organisation „Asien-Kontakt" hat die Hälfte meiner Reisekosten bezahlt. Diese Organisation will Kontakt zwischen Jugendlichen in Indien und Deutschland fördern — sowie auch Toleranz zwischen den beiden Ländern.

An meinem ersten Tag in der indischen Schule habe ich eine schöne Blumenkette bekommen — das ist ein Zeichen der Freundschaft. Wir hatten natürlich auch Geschenke und Infomaterial aus Deutschland mitgebracht.

Ich war sehr beeindruckt von der Gastfreundlichkeit unserer indischen Gastgeber. Sie haben so viele Ausflüge für uns organisiert, um uns das Land und Leute näher zu bringen, jeden Abend gab es ein richtiges Fest mit indischen Spezialitäten und wir haben sogar das indische Parlamentsgebäude in Neu Delhi besucht.

Für mich war es erstaunlich, dass sich so viele Leute in Indien für Deutschland und die Deutschen interessieren. In der Schule zeigten uns zwei Schülerinnen die Bücher, die sie ganz auf Deutsch gelesen hatten. Drei Jungen erzählten uns über die zwei Wochen, die sie bei einer Kirchengruppe in Hamburg verbracht hatten.

Nächstes Jahr möchte ich mit meiner Familie zurückfahren, um dieses schöne Land besser kennen zu lernen.

Questions

(a) In what way did the organisation *Asien-Kontakt* help Lisa Wiedermann?   1

Helped pay for the travel costs

MARKS | DO NOT WRITE IN THIS MARGIN

Text 2 Questions (continued)

(b) What does this organisation want to promote? State **two** things.   ②

Contact between youth in India and Germany

Build tolerance between both countries

(c) Why was Lisa given a necklace of flowers on her first day at the Indian school?   ①

It's a sign of friendship

(d) Lisa was impressed by Indian hospitality.

What did the Indian hosts arrange for the German visitors? State **three** things.   3   2

Brought the people and the country closer together.

every evening they had a feast of Indian specialties

and they visited the parliament in New Deli.

(e) What showed Lisa that Indian people have an interest in Germany?

Complete the sentences.   2   1

Two pupils showed her books which _were all in german_

_____.

Three boys told her about _the two weeks they spent in_

_Hamburg with a church group_____.

(f) Reading the passage as a whole, why do you think Lisa has chosen to write it?

Tick (✓) the correct box.   ①

She wants to move to India when she is older.	
She wants to promote understanding between the two countries.	✓
She wants to promote India as a holiday destination.	

Text 3

Sara, a German girl, is writing about her work placement and how to plan for the future.

Meine Lehrer in der Schule haben mir bei meiner Berufswahl sehr geholfen. Sie haben mit mir und meinen Eltern gesprochen, denn sie wissen, dass meine Noten in der Schule nicht immer gut sind. Sie sagen aber, dass ich eine gute Schülerin bin und das finde ich toll. Ich habe ein Arbeitspraktikum in einer Bäckerei gemacht und das hat großen Spaß gemacht. Die Arbeit ist sehr kreativ, man kann mit den Händen arbeiten, was ich sehr gut finde, und man kann auch mit neuen Ideen experimentieren. Als ich mein Praktikum machte, hatte ich eine gute Idee für einen Weihnachtskuchen und mein Chef hat gesagt: „Ja, warum nicht?" Mein Kuchen hat sehr gut geschmeckt und sie haben ihn in der Konditorei verkauft. Ich war so stolz.

Schon in der Schulzeit sollte man an eine künftige Karriere denken. Das ist nicht immer so einfach, denn man hat oft andere, wichtigere Dinge zu tun, wie zum Beispiel Prüfungen ablegen oder neue Talente entdecken und entwickeln. Viele Schüler fühlen sich einfach zu jung und unerfahren, um an ihre Berufswahl zu denken.

Ein Arbeitspraktikum ist aber eine gute Möglichkeit, Einblicke in die Arbeitswelt zu bekommen. Man kann durch eigene Erfahrung lernen und persönliche Kontakte schließen.

Questions

(a) Which of the following statements best describes Sara's work in school?

Tick (✓) the **one** correct statement.

1

Sara works well in school and is a high achiever.	
Sara's work is not perfect but she is a good pupil.	✓

(b) Why did Sara enjoy her work placement in the bakery? Give **three** reasons.

3

The work is very creative, you can work with your hands and experiment with new ideas

MARKS | DO NOT WRITE IN THIS MARGIN

Text 3 Questions (continued)

(c) Why was Sarah proud of her Christmas cake? State **two** things.   2   1

Her cake tasted very good and they sold it in the pastry shop

(d) What is often more important to school pupils than thinking about a future career? State **two** things.   2

thinking about exams and discover and develop new talents

(e) There are many advantages of doing a work placement. State any **two** of these.   2

A good opportunity to gain insights in the working world. You can get more contacts

[END OF QUESTION PAPER]

ADDITIONAL SPACE FOR ANSWERS

MARKS | DO NOT WRITE IN THIS MARGIN

ADDITIONAL SPACE FOR ANSWERS

[BLANK PAGE]

DO NOT WRITE ON THIS PAGE

N5

National
Qualifications
2015

Mark

X734/75/02

German
Writing

TUESDAY, 26 MAY
9:00 AM – 10:30 AM

Fill in these boxes and read what is printed below.

Full name of centre

Town

Forename(s)

Surname

Number of seat

Date of birth

Day	Month	Year	Scottish candidate number

Total marks — 20

Write your answer clearly, in **German**, in the space provided in this booklet.

You may use a German dictionary.

Additional space for answers is provided at the end of this booklet.

Use **blue** or **black** ink.

There is a separate question and answer booklet for Reading. You must complete your answers for Reading in the question and answer booklet for Reading.

Before leaving the examination room you must give both booklets to the Invigilator; if you do not, you may lose all the marks for this paper.

Total marks — 20

You are preparing an application for the job advertised below and you write an e-mail in **German** to the company.

Hotel „Sonnenhof"

Annagasse 15 — 90402 Nürnberg

Die Leitung des Hotels „Sonnenhof" sucht sofort freundliche, motivierte, junge Leute als

Mitarbeiter/-innen an der **Hotelrezeption**

Sie sollten gute Sprachkenntnisse in Englisch und Deutsch haben und sollten gut mit unseren Gästen umgehen können.

Sie können uns unter info@hotel-sonnenhof.de für weitere Information kontaktieren und uns Ihre Bewerbung schicken.

Ihre Bewerbung sollte folgende Information enthalten:

To help you to write your e-mail, you have been given the following checklist.

You must include **all** of these points:

- Personal details (name, age, where you live)
- School/college/education experience until now
- Skills/interests you have which make you right for the job
- Related work experience
- Any links you may have with a German-speaking country
- Your future education/career plans

Use all of the above to help you write the e-mail in **German**. The e-mail should be approximately 120–150 words. You may use a German dictionary.

ANSWER SPACE

Halo! Mein Name ist Hannah Cowan, ich bin fünfzehn Jahre alt und ich wohne in einen ruhigen Dorf, das Fortrose heißt. Ich wohne seit zwölf Jahren hier, weil ich von Edinburg umgezogen bin.

Ich gehe auf eine Gesamtschule die Fortrose Academy, heißt. Ich lerne seit zwei Jahren Deutsch und ich genieße es wirklich! Ich finde es gut, eine Fremdsprache zu lernen, weil man seine Arbeitsmöglichkeiten erweitern kann. Wenn ich die Schule verlasse werde ich auf die Universität gehen, um Linguistik zu studieren.

Meine Lehrer sagen, dass ich sehr fleißig und ehrlich bin. Ich werde mich freuen, meine Fähigkeiten beweisen zu können. * Ich komme gut mit allen aus und ich finde es gut! * Letzten Jahr war ich in Bayern für acht Tage und ich möchte das Land besser kennen lernen.

Ich habe keinen Nebenjob aber in den Sommerferien gearbeitet letzten Jahr habe ich in die Bibliothek. Dort, habe ich Bücher organisiert und Ich habe auch Empfehlung gegeben. Es war ein tolles erlebnis und ich habe viele gelernt!

ANSWER SPACE (continued)

Letzten Jahr bin ich mit den schule nach Deutschland gefahren. Es war ein Austach und es hat sehr spaß gemacht! Mein Parterin heißt Antonia und sie war sehr nett. Wir haben Munich, Augsberg und Neuschwanstein besucht!

Meiner Meinung nach Linguistik sind sehr interessant. Ich möchte nach Heriot Watt gehen zum es studieren wenn ich die schule verlassen. Es ist sehr nützlich, dass ich fließend in English und Gälisch bin!

ANSWER SPACE (continued)

MARKS | DO NOT WRITE IN THIS MARGIN

ANSWER SPACE (continued)

[END OF QUESTION PAPER]

MARKS | DO NOT WRITE IN THIS MARGIN

ADDITIONAL SPACE FOR ANSWERS

Page seven

MARKS DO NOT WRITE IN THIS MARGIN

ADDITIONAL SPACE FOR ANSWERS

National
Qualifications
2015

Mark 15/20
75 %

X734/75/03

**German
Listening**

TUESDAY, 26 MAY

10:50 AM – 11:15 AM (approx)

Fill in these boxes and read what is printed below.

Full name of centre

Town

Forename(s)

Surname

Number of seat

Date of birth
Day   Month   Year   Scottish candidate number

Total marks — 20

Attempt ALL questions.

You will hear two items in German. **Before you hear each item, you will have one minute to study the questions.** You will hear each item three times, with an interval of one minute between playings. You will then have time to answer the questions before hearing the next item.

You may NOT use a German dictionary.

Write your answers clearly, in **English**, in the spaces provided in this booklet. Additional space for answers is provided at the end of this booklet. If you use this space you must clearly identify the question number you are attempting.

Use **blue** or **black** ink.

You are not allowed to leave the examination room until the end of the test.

Before leaving the examination room you must give this booklet to the Invigilator; if you do not, you may lose all the marks for this paper.

MARKS | DO NOT WRITE IN THIS MARGIN

Total marks — 20

Attempt ALL questions

Item 1

Erik is talking about life at home and why he has two bedrooms.

(a) When is Erik's birthday? Tick (✓) the correct box. **1**

3rd August	
13th August	✓
31st August	

(b) When did Erik's parents separate? **1**

4 years ago, when he was 11 years old.

(c) When does Erik live with his father? State any **two** things. **2**

Wednesdays and holidays.

(d) What are the arrangements for Erik at Christmas? State **two** things. **2**

He spends them with his mum, his father visits 2 days after

(e) Why is Maths Erik's favourite subject? **1**

He gets good marks

(f) Overall, how does Erik feel about life at the moment?
Tick (✓) the most appropriate statement. **1**

He is unhappy.	
He has his ups and downs.	✓
He is positive.	

Page two

Item 2

Erik continues in an interview.

MARKS

DO NOT WRITE IN THIS MARGIN

(a) Who is Martin?   1

His little brother

(b) What does he say about his relationship with Martin?
State any **one** thing.   1

They get on well

(c) What do Erik's parents do for a living? Complete the grid.   2

| Mother | Secretary in an office. |
| Father | Politician |

(d) Why can't Erik and Martin have a dog?   1

His mother is allergic

(e) (i) **Apart from** electric guitar, what instrument does Erik play?   1

Piano

     (ii) How long has he been playing this instrument?   1

3 years

(f) What does Erik say about his friends at school? State any **three** things.   3

They're often quite loud, funny and they have the same interests. He has three or four close friends

(g) What do Erik and his friend do in their spare time? State any **two** things.   2

Play sport together and go to the cinema.

[END OF QUESTION PAPER]

MARKS | DO NOT WRITE IN THIS MARGIN

ADDITIONAL SPACE FOR ANSWERS

MARKS | DO NOT WRITE IN THIS MARGIN

ADDITIONAL SPACE FOR ANSWERS

[BLANK PAGE]

DO NOT WRITE ON THIS PAGE

National
Qualifications
2015

X734/75/13

German
Listening Transcript

TUESDAY, 26 MAY

10:50 AM – 11:15 AM

This paper must not be seen by any candidate.

The material overleaf is provided for use in an emergency only (eg the recording or equipment proving faulty) or where permission has been given in advance by SQA for the material to be read to candidates with additional support needs. The material must be read exactly as printed.

Instructions to reader(s):

For each item, read the English once, then read the German **three times**, with an interval of 1 minute between the three readings. On completion of the third reading, pause for the length of time indicated in brackets after the item, to allow the candidates to write their answers.

Where special arrangements have been agreed in advance to allow the reading of the material, those sections marked **(f)** should be read by a female speaker and those marked **(m)** by a male; those sections marked **(t)** should be read by the teacher.

(t)   Item number one.

Erik is talking about life at home and why he has two bedrooms.

You now have one minute to study the questions for Item number one.

(m) Mein Name ist Erik und ich bin 15. Ich habe am 13. August Geburtstag. Ich wohne in einem Haus in Nürnberg-Galgenhof — das ist ein Vorort von Nürnberg. Ich habe zwei Schlafzimmer, das eine bei meiner Mutter hier in Nürnberg und das zweite bei meinem Vater in Fürth. Fürth liegt nur acht Kilometer von Nürnberg entfernt.

Meine Eltern haben sich vor vier Jahren getrennt, als ich elf Jahre alt war. Ich lebe die meiste Zeit bei meiner Mutter. Aber mittwochs, jedes zweite Wochenende und vier Wochen in den Schulferien wohne ich bei meinem Vater und seiner Freundin.

Ich verbringe Weihnachten immer bei meiner Mutter. Meinen Vater besuche ich immer zwei Tage später. So bekomme ich zweimal Geschenke. Das ist toll!

Ich gehe in die zehnte Klasse eines Gymnasiums in Nürnberg. Am besten gefallen mir die Fächer Kunst, Musik und Mathe. Mathe ist mein Lieblingsfach und ich bekomme immer gute Noten. Und natürlich auch Sport! Außerdem spiele ich Fußball und Volleyball im Verein.

(2 minutes)

(t) Item number two.

Erik continues in an interview.

You now have one minute to study the questions for Item number two.

(f) Erik, hast du Geschwister?

(m) Ja, zu Hause sind wir zu dritt. Meine Mutter, mein kleiner Bruder Martin und ich. Martin ist zwei Jahre jünger als ich.

(f) Kommst du mit Martin gut aus?

(m) Ja, klar! Wir kommen miteinander ganz gut aus — er kann mir ab und zu auf die Nerven gehen, zum Beispiel, wenn er in mein Zimmer kommt, ohne an die Tür zu klopfen, aber ich mag ihn.

(f) Was machen deine Eltern beruflich?

(m) Meine Mutter ist Sekretärin in einem Büro in der Stadtmitte und mein Vater ist Polizist. Meine Mutter ist klein und schlank. Sie hat blonde Haare und grüne Augen. Mein Vater ist 42 und meine Mutter ist zwei Jahre jünger.

(f) Habt ihr Haustiere?

(m) Ja, wir haben zwei Goldfische. Martin und ich möchten sehr gerne einen Hund, aber meine Mutter ist gegen Hunde allergisch!

(f) Du interessierst dich für Musik. Spielst du ein Instrument?

(m) Ja, ich spiele seit drei Jahren Klavier und seit einem Jahr elektrische Gitarre. Ich gehe mit zwei Freunden zur Musikgruppe in der Stadtmitte, wo wir zusammen Musik machen.

(f) Hast du viele Freunde in der Schule?

(m) Ja, ich habe drei oder vier echt gute Freunde. Sie sind oft ziemlich laut, aber ich finde sie auch sehr lustig und wir haben die gleichen Interessen.

(f) Treibt ihr auch viel Sport?

(m) Ja, wir gehen zusammen im Stadtpark joggen, machen in der Gegend Radtouren und spielen in der Fußballmannschaft der Schule — ich bin Stürmer. Wir gehen auch regelmäßig ins Kino.

(f) Was für Filme seht ihr gerne?

(m) Wir sehen uns gern Abenteuerfilme an. Mein Lieblingsschauspieler ist Will Smith und mein Lieblingsfilm ist «X-Men».

(f) Danke, Erik!

(m) Kein Problem!

(2 minutes)

(t) **End of test.**

Now look over your answers.

[END OF TRANSCRIPT]

[BLANK PAGE]

DO NOT WRITE ON THIS PAGE

NATIONAL 5

2016

N5

National
Qualifications
2016

Mark

X734/75/01

German
Reading

WEDNESDAY, 1 JUNE
1:00 PM – 2:30 PM

Fill in these boxes and read what is printed below.

Full name of centre

Town

Forename(s)

Surname

Number of seat

Date of birth

Day	Month	Year

Scottish candidate number

Total marks — 30

Attempt ALL questions.

Write your answers clearly, in **English**, in the spaces provided in this booklet.

You may use a German dictionary.

Additional space for answers is provided at the end of this booklet. If you use this space you must clearly identify the question number you are attempting.

Use **blue** or **black** ink.

There is a separate question and answer booklet for Writing. You must complete your answer for Writing in the question and answer booklet for Writing.

Before leaving the examination room you must give this booklet to the Invigilator; if you do not, you may lose all the marks for this paper.

Total marks — 30

Attempt ALL questions

Text 1

You read an online article explaining what citizens in Munich can do to help protect the environment.

Wie kann man als Bürger hier in München mehr für die Umwelt tun? Hier einige Tipps, wie man unseren Planeten schützen kann.

Kostenlose Zeitungen und unerwünschte Broschüren im Briefkasten bedeuten eine Verschwendung von Rohstoffen. Ein Aufkleber an der Haustür, der sagt „STOP — Bitte keine Werbung", ist eine billige und wirksame Lösung.

In München gibt es heute immer mehr Geschäfte, wo man Bio-Obst und -Gemüse kaufen kann. Hier muss man aber vorsichtig sein, denn Bio-Kiwis aus Neuseeland oder Bio-Äpfel aus Argentinien werden mit dem Flugzeug nach Deutschland transportiert und deswegen gibt es so viel Luftverschmutzung.

Wenn man etwas braucht, ist es nicht immer nötig, etwas Neues zu kaufen. Wenn man zum Beispiel einen neuen Tisch braucht, kann man einen alten Tisch auf einem Flohmarkt kaufen. Das sieht oft besser aus und ist normalerweise preiswerter.

Studenten an der Uni können sich oft gegenseitig helfen. Man kann zum Beispiel Kleider austauschen, und man kann andere Sachen wie Sportartikel teilen.

Es ist auch gut, wenn man versucht, kaputte Dinge zu reparieren. Wenn man ein Fahrrad oder eine Waschmaschine reparieren kann, ist das viel besser als etwas Neues zu kaufen. Jedes Jahr in Deutschland landen 500.000 Tonnen Elektrogeräte auf dem Schrotthaufen und das ist viel zu viel.

Questions

(a) What does the article say about junk mail? Complete the sentence. **1**

Free newspapers and unwanted brochures are a waste of

raw materials .

(b) What is a good and cheap way of stopping this junk mail? **1**

Put a sticker on the house door that says 'Stop - no advertising please.'

MARKS | DO NOT WRITE IN THIS MARGIN

Text 1 Questions (continued)

(c) Why do you have to be careful when buying organic fruit from countries such as Argentina and New Zealand? State **two** things. — 2

They're transported to Germany via planes and therefore they cause a lot of air pollution

(d) What are the benefits of buying an old table instead of a brand new one? State **two** things. — 2

They often look better and ^are normally cheaper.

(e) What can students at the university do to help? State **two** things. — 2

They could exchange clothes and share other things like sports equipment.

(f) (i) There is a final suggestion on how to help the environment. What is this? — 1

Repair things such as bikes and washing machines instead of buying new ones.

(ii) What statistic supports this suggestion at the end of the article? Complete the sentence. — 1

500,000 tonnes of _electrical appliances._
land on the scrapheap each year.

[Turn over

Text 2

You are browsing a German online magazine when the following article about an interesting school catches your eye.

Bis vor kurzem haben fast keine Schüler des Sophie Scholl Gymnasiums in München in der Schulkantine gegessen. Das Essen war wenig schmackhaft. Die Schüler gingen lieber in Fastfood-Restaurants, aber das Essen in diesen Restaurants enthält oft viel Fett.

Die Schüler haben aber eine Lösung zu diesem Problem gefunden: Sie kochen selbst jeden Tag. Alle zwei Wochen ist eine andere Klasse für das Mittagessen verantwortlich.

Der Schuldirektor findet das Projekt wichtig für die Gesundheit der Schüler. Die meisten Kinder haben ihre Essgewohnheiten geändert. Wenn sie abends nach Hause kommen, wird das Essen nicht mehr im Mikrowellenherd aufgewärmt. Die Schüler haben jetzt Lust, mit frischen Zutaten zu kochen.

Weil die Schüler so viel in der Schule machen müssen, lernen sie Verantwortung zu übernehmen. Sie lernen auch etwas über die Zusammenarbeit mit anderen und auch wie viel die Lebensmittel kosten.

Das Projekt hat viel Erfolg gehabt. Mehr Schüler essen jetzt in der Kantine. Das Schulessen ist jetzt lecker und viel gesünder. Es gibt noch einen Vorteil — die Schüler können eine zweite Portion kostenlos bekommen.

Questions

(a) What does the article say about eating habits at the Sophie Scholl Gymnasium? Complete the sentences.   2

Until recently _almost no_ pupils ate in the school canteen.

The food was _not healthy_ .

(b) What solution have the pupils found to this problem? State **two** things.   2

They cook themselves and every two weeks another class has the responsibility of lunch

MARKS | DO NOT WRITE IN THIS MARGIN

Text 2 Questions (continued)

(c) In what ways have eating habits for pupils changed at home? State **two** things.

2

_____

_____

(d) What have the pupils learned as a result of this project? State any **two** things.

2

_____

_____

(e) Give **two** reasons why more pupils are now eating in the canteen.

2

_____

_____

[Turn over

MARKS | DO NOT WRITE IN THIS MARGIN

Text 3

You read an article about starting your own business.

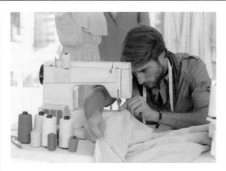

Heute wollen immer mehr Leute eine eigene Firma gründen. Das bringt sicher viele Vorteile mit sich — man kann immer das machen, was man will. Man ist selbst für Zeitmanagement verantwortlich und man hat die Chance, eigene Ideen zu entwickeln.

Manfred Schultz ist heute Inhaber einer kleinen Textilfirma. Die Idee hatte er, als er Student war: „Ich hatte begonnen, meine eigenen Kleider zu machen und ich habe sie auf dem Sonntagsmarkt in der Stadt verkauft. Sehr viele Studenten haben meine Kleider gekauft, und bald begann ich sie in der Stadt zu sehen. Das hat mich ermutigt, weiterzumachen!

Am Ende meiner Studienzeit hatte ich genug Geld für einen Gebrauchtwagen und für eine achtwöchige Reise durch ganz Italien. Später habe ich ein kleines Geschäft in meiner Heimatstadt eröffnet.

So einfach ist es aber nicht. Man muss an die Nebenkosten denken: Man braucht eine Versicherung und man muss oft eine Nähmaschine reparieren lassen.

Natürlich muss man auch mit Enttäuschungen rechnen. Viele Leute finden das schwierig. Ich hatte zum Beispiel gehofft, dass ein großes Warenhaus meine Kleider kaufen würde, aber am Ende wollten sie meine Jacken und Hemden verändern und das war für mich absolut inakzeptabel. Trotzdem bin ich immer noch zufrieden mit der Arbeit."

Questions

(a) According to the article, what are the advantages of starting your own business? State any **two** things.   2

_____

_____

(b) (i) Where did Manfred Schultz first sell the clothes he had made?   1

_____

(ii) What things encouraged him to keep going? State **two** things.   2

_____

_____

MARKS | DO NOT WRITE IN THIS MARGIN

Text 3 Questions (continued)

(c) What did Manfred do when his studies were finished? State any **two** things.

2

_____

_____

(d) There are many additional costs involved in running a business. Give any **one** example of these.

1

_____

(e) Why did Manfred reject the chance to have his designs in a big department store?

1

_____

(f) What general view does this article give of running your own business? Tick (✓) the correct box.

1

	Tick (✓)
It's something that anyone can do.	
It's worthwhile, although there are also difficulties.	
It's just not worth all the effort.	

[END OF QUESTION PAPER]

MARKS

DO NOT
WRITE IN
THIS
MARGIN

ADDITIONAL SPACE FOR ANSWERS

MARKS

DO NOT WRITE IN THIS MARGIN

ADDITIONAL SPACE FOR ANSWERS

[BLANK PAGE]

DO NOT WRITE ON THIS PAGE

N5

National
Qualifications
2016

Mark

X734/75/02

German
Writing

WEDNESDAY, 1 JUNE
1:00 PM – 2:30 PM

Fill in these boxes and read what is printed below.

Full name of centre

Town

Forename(s)

Surname

Number of seat

Date of birth

Day	Month	Year		Scottish candidate number

Total marks — 20

Write your answer clearly, in **German**, in the space provided in this booklet.

You may use a German dictionary.

Additional space for answers is provided at the end of this booklet.

Use **blue** or **black** ink.

There is a separate question and answer booklet for Reading. You must complete your answers for Reading in the question and answer booklet for Reading.

Before leaving the examination room you must give this booklet to the Invigilator; if you do not, you may lose all the marks for this paper.

MARKS | DO NOT WRITE IN THIS MARGIN

Total marks — 20

You are preparing an application for the job advertised below and you write an e-mail in **German** to the company.

Gaststube "Rheinblick"

Flußweg 3,
55422 Bacharach,
Rheinland-Pfalz

Wir suchen für unser Restaurant **einen Kellner/eine Kellnerin.**

Sind Sie fleißig, motiviert und höflich?

Haben Sie gute Englisch- und Deutschkenntnisse?

Schicken Sie Ihre Bewerbung an:

info@gaststube.rheinblick.de

To help you to write your e-mail, you have been given the following checklist.
You must include **all** of these points:

- Personal details (name, age, where you live)
- School/college/education experience until now
- Skills/interests you have which make you right for the job
- Related work experience
- Any previous links with Germany or a German-speaking country
- Any questions related to the job

Use all of the above to help you write the e-mail in **German**. The e-mail should be approximately 120—150 words. You may use a German dictionary.

MARKS | DO NOT WRITE IN THIS MARGIN

ANSWER SPACE

ANSWER SPACE (continued)

MARKS | DO NOT WRITE IN THIS MARGIN

ANSWER SPACE (continued)

MARKS | DO NOT WRITE IN THIS MARGIN

ANSWER SPACE (continued)

[END OF QUESTION PAPER]

MARKS DO NOT WRITE IN THIS MARGIN

ADDITIONAL SPACE FOR ANSWERS

MARKS DO NOT WRITE IN THIS MARGIN

ADDITIONAL SPACE FOR ANSWERS

FOR OFFICIAL USE

N5

National
Qualifications
2016

Mark

X734/75/03

**German
Listening**

WEDNESDAY, 1 JUNE
2:50 PM — 3:20 PM (approx)

Fill in these boxes and read what is printed below.

Full name of centre

Town

Forename(s)

Surname

Number of seat

Date of birth

Day   Month   Year

Scottish candidate number

Total marks — 20

Attempt ALL questions.

You will hear two items in German. **Before you hear each item, you will have one minute to study the questions.** You will hear each item three times, with an interval of one minute between playings. You will then have time to answer the questions before hearing the next item.

You may NOT use a German dictionary.

Write your answers clearly, in **English**, in the spaces provided in this booklet. Additional space for answers is provided at the end of this booklet. If you use this space you must clearly identify the question number you are attempting.

Use **blue** or **black** ink.

You are not allowed to leave the examination room until the end of the test.

Before leaving the examination room you must give this booklet to the Invigilator; if you do not, you may lose all the marks for this paper.

MARKS | DO NOT WRITE IN THIS MARGIN

Total marks — 20

Attempt ALL questions

Item 1

Evelyn Hirsch, from Hamburg, is talking about spending holidays with friends.

(a) What kind of accommodation do people choose when on holiday with friends? State any **two** things.

2

_____

_____

(b) Evelyn gives various reasons for spending holidays with friends. State any **one** of these.

1

_____

(c) Where exactly did Evelyn and her husband rent a villa last year with their friends?

1

_____

(d) Where did they find the accommodation?

1

_____

(e) What does Evelyn enjoy doing on holiday? State any **two** things.

2

_____

_____

(f) What is Evelyn's personal view on holidays with friends? Tick (✓) the correct statement.

1

	Tick (✓)
It's the only way to get the most out of a holiday.	
She's tried it and won't do it again.	
She's looking forward to doing it again.	

MARKS |

Item 2

Evelyn and her husband Rolf are discussing their plans for this year's holiday.

(a) Why does Rolf want to go on holiday to Italy? Complete the following sentence.

1

Rolf wants to go to Italy because _____ recommended it to him.

(b) What reasons does Evelyn give for wanting to stay in Germany for the holidays? State any **two**.

2

_____

_____

(c) Why does Rolf not want to spend a holiday in a town? Give any **one** reason.

1

_____

(d) Where in Germany does Evelyn suggest that they could spend this year's holiday?

1

_____

(e) Why does Rolf not want to go there? State any **one** reason.

1

_____

(f) Why does Rolf suggest a holiday in Austria? Complete the following sentences.

2

Rolf wants to go to Austria because _____ .

It's beautiful and _____ .

(g) What puts Evelyn off going to Austria this year? State any **one** thing.

1

_____

(h) Rolf says Edinburgh is a wonderful place. Why else does he want to go there?

1

_____

[Turn over

MARKS

Item 2 (continued)

(i)   Where do they finally decide to spend this year's holiday?   1

_____

(j)   What job will they do while on holiday?   1

_____

[END OF QUESTION PAPER]

MARKS | DO NOT WRITE IN THIS MARGIN

ADDITIONAL SPACE FOR ANSWERS

Page five

MARKS

ADDITIONAL SPACE FOR ANSWERS

National Qualifications 2016

X734/75/13

German Listening Transcript

WEDNESDAY, 1 JUNE

2:50 PM — 3:20 PM (approx)

This paper must not be seen by any candidate.

The material overleaf is provided for use in an emergency only (eg the recording or equipment proving faulty) or where permission has been given in advance by SQA for the material to be read to candidates with additional support needs. The material must be read exactly as printed.

Instructions to reader(s):

For each item, read the English once, then read the German **three times**, with an interval of 1 minute between the three playings. On completion of the third reading, pause for the length of time indicated in brackets after the item, to allow the candidates to write their answers.

Where special arrangements have been agreed in advance to allow the reading of the material, those sections marked **(f)** should be read by a female speaker and those marked **(m)** by a male; those sections marked **(t)** should be read by the teacher.

(t) Item Number One

Evelyn Hirsch, from Hamburg, is talking about spending holidays with friends.

You now have one minute to study the questions for Item Number One.

(f) Sehr viele Deutsche fahren jedes Jahr in den Urlaub und Millionen von uns verbringen gern Ferien mit Freunden. Wir mieten ein Strandhaus auf Korfu, eine Ferienwohnung in Spanien oder wir verbringen Zeit in einem Wohnwagen in den Alpen.

Ja, solche Ferien mit Freunden sind sehr beliebt und es gibt viele Gründe dafür: Man kann zusammenwohnen und die Arbeit teilen, zum Beispiel das Kochen und Abwaschen. Es ist viel billiger als im Hotel und viele Leute haben Freunde, die vielleicht eine andere Sprache sprechen können. Für uns war es aber ganz anders.

Mein Mann und ich sind letztes Jahr nach Südfrankreich gefahren und wir haben eine Ferienvilla mit unseren Freunden Lars und Annette geteilt. Die Villa haben wir in einer Ferienbroschüre gefunden. Von Anfang an war es eine absolute Katastrophe.

Im Urlaub liege ich sehr gern in der Sonne, schwimme im Meer oder ich gehe gern ins große Einkaufszentrum in der nächsten Stadt. Mein Mann Rolf verbringt am liebsten Zeit in der Kunstgalerie. Letztes Jahr konnten wir das nicht machen, weil unsere Freunde auch da waren. Nächstes Jahr fahren wir allein in den Urlaub.

(2 minutes)

(t) Item Number Two

Evelyn and her husband Rolf are discussing their plans for this year's holiday.

You now have one minute to study the questions for Item Number Two.

(m) Ich möchte dieses Jahr die Ferien in Italien verbringen. Meine Chefin war letztes Jahr da und sie meint, dass das Land sehr schön sei, und die Leute sehr freundlich.

(f) Schon gut Rolf, aber Ferien im Ausland sind nicht immer was für mich. Man kann auch hier in Deutschland bleiben und gute Ferien haben. Man kann überall mit dem Auto hinfahren und man kann das Land besser kennen lernen.

(m) Ich will unter keinen Umständen meine Ferien in einer Stadt verbringen. Im Urlaub will ich Hektik und Stress vergessen. Für mich ist die Ruhe sehr wichtig.

(f) Ja, vielleicht hast du Recht. Wie wär's mit einem kleinen Ferienhaus an der Nordseeküste?

(m) Nee. Das ist auch keine gute Idee. Du weißt ja, dass das Wetter da oft furchtbar ist. Ich war letztes Jahr in Norddeutschland und es hat die ganze Zeit geregnet.

(f) Ja gut, dann ist ein Urlaub in der Stadt perfekt, weil es immer viel zu tun gibt, auch wenn das Wetter nicht gut ist.

(m) Wir könnten einen Kompromiss finden. Warum fahren wir nicht nach Österreich? Es ist nicht zu weit weg, die Landschaft ist wunderschön, und so teuer ist es auch nicht. Was meinst du?

(f) Österreich ist sicher ein sehr schönes Land, aber ich will da nicht hinfahren. Ich war vor zwei Jahren mit meiner Schwester da. Es war ganz gut, aber ich will etwas Neues erleben. Hast du vergessen?

(m) Wir könnten vielleicht eine Woche in Schottland verbringen. Edinburg soll eine wunderbare Stadt sein, und die Einkaufsmöglichkeiten sind super.

(f) Aber Rolf, du wolltest doch keine Stadtferien. Edinburg ist ja die Hauptstadt von Schottland und es gibt sicher viele Touristen im Sommer da.

(m) Mmm, vielleicht hast du Recht Evelyn. Ich glaube, wir werden dieses Jahr zu Hause bleiben. Wir können dadurch Geld sparen und wir müssen endlich die Zeit finden, die Garage aufzuräumen.

(2 minutes)

(t) End of test.

Now look over your answers.

[END OF TRANSCRIPT]

[BLANK PAGE]

DO NOT WRITE ON THIS PAGE

NATIONAL 5

2017

National
Qualifications
2017

Mark 2⁷/₃₀

X734/75/01

German
Reading

FRIDAY, 2 JUNE
1:00 PM – 2:30 PM

Fill in these boxes and read what is printed below.

Full name of centre

Town

Forename(s)

Hannah

Surname

Cavan

Number of seat

Date of birth

Day	Month	Year	Scottish candidate number

Total marks — 30

Attempt ALL questions.

Write your answers clearly, in **English**, in the spaces provided in this booklet.

You may use a German dictionary.

Additional space for answers is provided at the end of this booklet. If you use this space you must clearly identify the question number you are attempting.

Use **blue** or **black** ink.

There is a separate question and answer booklet for Writing. You must complete your answer for Writing in the question and answer booklet for Writing.

Before leaving the examination room you must give both booklets to the Invigilator; if you do not, you may lose all the marks for this paper.

Total marks — 30

Attempt ALL questions

Text 1

You read an article about a young woman who has learned to fly a plane.

> **Diese starke Frau kennt keine Grenzen**
>
> Jessica Cox ist der erste Mensch ohne Arme, der den Pilotenschein gemacht hat. Mit einem strahlenden Lächeln steigt Jessica nach dem Flug aus dem Flieger. „Fliegen ist das beste Gefühl der Welt", schwärmt sie. Das Besondere daran — Jessica wurde ohne Arme geboren. Sie steuert das Flugzeug mit den Füßen.
>
> Nach dreijähriger Ausbildung und entgegen allen Erwartungen hat Jessica ihren Pilotenschein endlich bekommen. Als Jessica ihren Eltern am Anfang gesagt hat, dass sie Pilotin werden möchte, haben sie sich Sorgen gemacht und Bedenken gehegt. Trotzdem haben sie Jessica unterstützt, um die Herausforderungen zu überwinden.
>
> Jessica hat jetzt viel mehr Zeit für sich nach dem Ende ihrer Ausbildung und nutzt ihre Freizeit völlig aus. Jede Woche geht sie mit Freunden klettern. Außerdem ist sie seit mehreren Jahren Mitglied im Segelverein und verbringt jedes zweite Wochenende am Meer.
>
> Jessica ist für alle jungen Leute ein tolles Vorbild und sie will jetzt andere Teenager ermutigen, ihre Wünsche und Träume zu erfüllen. Sie hat im Fernsehen viele Interviews gegeben und in ihrer alten Schule über ihre Abenteuer gesprochen. Sie hat auch kostenlose Flüge für behinderte Kinder organisiert. Damit wollte sie ihnen zeigen, dass alles möglich ist.
>
> „Man sollte nie aufgeben. Ich habe gelernt, meinen Traum zu leben und nicht mein Leben zu träumen. Das kann jeder auch," meint Jessica.

Questions

(a) In what way does Jessica describe flying in the first paragraph? **1**

It's the best feeling in the world

(b) What makes Jessica's achievement unique? State **two** things. **2**

• First person without arms to become a pilot

• She controls the plane with her feet

MARKS | DO NOT WRITE IN THIS MARGIN

Text 1 Questions (continued)

(c) What was her parents' reaction when she first told them she wanted to be a pilot? State any **two** things. (2)

· They were concerned

· They were supportive

(d) In what ways does Jessica spend her free time? State any **two** things. 2 | 1

· Every week she goes climbing with her friends

· Spends every second weekend at sea

(e) What has Jessica done to encourage other teenagers to fulfil their dreams? State any **two** things. (2)

· Been on Interviews on the TV

· Organised free flights for children with special needs

(f) Jessica gives advice at the end of the article. What advice does she give? State any **one** thing. (1)

You should never give up

[Turn over

MARKS | DO NOT WRITE IN THIS MARGIN

Text 2

You read an article about outdoor learning at a primary school near Berlin.

Einmal im Monat haben die Schüler der Beethoven-Grundschule draußen in dem benachbarten Wald Unterricht.

Maria Schneider, eine Lehrerin der Schule, behauptet, dass der Unterricht draußen in der Natur viele Vorteile mit sich bringt. ,,Die Schüler lernen die örtliche Umgebung und die Natur besser kennen. Sie benutzen alle ihre Sinne, um über den natürlichen Lebensraum von Insekten, Pflanzen und Tieren zu lernen. Outdoor-Lernen ist ein sehr wichtiges Erlebnis für alle Kinder.“

Der zwölfjährige Thorsten Bachmann mag es sehr, im Freien zu lernen. ,,Ich hasse es, wenn man im Klassenraum sitzen muss, während draußen die Sonne scheint. Ich arbeite gern mit meinen Freunden, um Rätsel zusammen zu lösen und Spiele zusammen zu spielen. Am meisten Spaß macht es, etwas über Tiere zu lernen. Letzte Woche entdeckten wir die Muster in der Natur: die Blütenblätter, die Adern eines Blattes und die Rinde eines Baumes.“

Outdoor-Lernen ist auch gut für die Gesundheit. Draußen sein bedeutet, dass die Schüler Zeit an der frischen Luft verbringen dürfen, sich regelmäßig bewegen und ihre Immunsysteme stärken. Die vermehrte Menge an Sauerstoff im Körper hilft den Schülern, sich besser konzentrieren zu können.

Jedoch muss der Unterricht manchmal kurzfristig abgesagt werden, weil das Wetter nicht immer zuverlässig ist.

Questions

(a) Where do the pupils at the *Beethoven-Grundschule* have their lessons once a month?

1

·In the neighbouring forrest

(b) Maria Schneider is a teacher at the school. What advantages of outdoor learning does she mention? State any **two** things.

2

·Understand nature better

·They use all their senses to learn about the natural habitat of insects, plants and animals

MARKS | DO NOT WRITE IN THIS MARGIN

Text 2 Questions (continued)

(c) Why does Thorsten Bachmann enjoy learning outdoors? State any **two** things.

2

· He hates it when he's in the classroom and the sun is shining. · He finds learning about animals fun

(d) What patterns in nature did he discover last week? State any **two** things.

2

· The veins of a leaf
· Bark from a tree

(e) In what ways is outdoor learning good for pupils' health? State any **two** things.

2

· They spend time in the fresh air
· It strengthens their immune system.

(f) Why do the lessons sometimes need to be cancelled at short notice? Complete the sentence:

The lessons sometimes need to be cancelled at short notice because the

weather is not always reliable .

1

[Turn over

Text 3

You read an article online about the advantages of taking a gap year after school.

Letztes Jahr haben fast ein Drittel der deutschen Schulabsolventen zwischen Schule und Studium oder Ausbildung ein Brückenjahr genommen. Das Brückenjahr ermöglicht vielen Jugendlichen, etwas Ungewöhnliches und Lohnendes zu unternehmen, Arbeitserfahrung zu sammeln, die Welt zu bereisen und neue Länder und Kulturen zu entdecken.

Viele Universitäten und Berufsschulen ermutigen Schulabsolventen, sich ein Jahr frei zu nehmen. Sie sind sich einig, dass dieses Jahr sich positiv auf die neuen Studenten auswirkt, weil sie sich dadurch besser auf die neuen Herausforderungen an der Uni vorbereiten. Max Weber, ein Dozent an der Uni Bonn, berichtet, dass „ein Brückenjahr eine wertvolle Erfahrung für die meisten Studenten ist. Die Studenten sind normalerweise fokussierter, haben nützliche Lebenserfahrungen und entwickeln einen starken Charakter. Gute Noten in der Schule sind nicht mehr genug, um an der Uni erfolgreich zu sein."

Außerdem ist die Erfahrung aus dem Brückenjahr sehr hilfreich, wenn man sich für einen Job bewirbt. Arbeitgeber suchen immer nach Kandidaten mit interessanten Lebensläufen und Bewerbungen. Die Erfahrung aus dem Brückenjahr kann in Vorstellungsgesprächen sehr nützlich sein. Arbeitgeber wollen, dass man echte Beispiele nennt, wie:

- wann man Initiative gezeigt hat
- wann man unter Druck gearbeitet hat
- wann man in einem Team gearbeitet hat
- wann man Verantwortung übernommen hat.

Ein Brückenjahr ermöglicht es den Bewerbern, aus der Masse herauszuragen* und es schafft ihnen einen Vorsprung in allen Bewerbungsgesprächen.

*herausragen — to stand out

Questions

(a) How many German school leavers took a gap year last year? **1**

Almost one third

MARKS | DO NOT WRITE IN THIS MARGIN

Text 3 Questions (continued)

(b) Why do many German school leavers take a gap year? State any **two** things.

2

· To do something unusual and rewarding.

· To travel the world and discover new cultures

(c) Universities and colleges encourage school leavers to take a gap year. Why is this? Complete the following sentence:

A gap year is positive for new students, as they are better prepared for

the ____challenge____ at university.

1

(d) What does Max Weber say about students who have taken a gap year? State any **two** things.

2

· They are more focused

· They get good marks in school

(e) Gap year experience is also beneficial when applying for a job. What are employers always looking for?

1

· Candidates with interesting CVs and
applications

(f) Employers want candidates to provide real examples in interviews. What types of examples are they looking for? State any **three** things.

3

· Good at working in a Team

· Work well under pressure

· Can take responsibility.

[END OF QUESTION PAPER]

MARKS DO NOT WRITE IN THIS MARGIN

ADDITIONAL SPACE FOR ANSWERS

MARKS

DO NOT WRITE IN THIS MARGIN

ADDITIONAL SPACE FOR ANSWERS

[BLANK PAGE]

DO NOT WRITE ON THIS PAGE

[BLANK PAGE]

DO NOT WRITE ON THIS PAGE

[BLANK PAGE]

DO NOT WRITE ON THIS PAGE

N5

National
Qualifications
2017

Mark

X734/75/02

German
Writing

FRIDAY, 2 JUNE
1:00 PM – 2:30 PM

Fill in these boxes and read what is printed below.

Full name of centre

Town

Forename(s)

Surname

Number of seat

Date of birth

Day

Month

Year

Scottish candidate number

Total marks — 20

Write your answer clearly, in **German**, in the space provided in this booklet.

You may use a German dictionary.

Additional space for answers is provided at the end of this booklet.

Use **blue** or **black** ink.

There is a separate question and answer booklet for Reading. You must complete your answers for Reading in the question and answer booklet for Reading.

Before leaving the examination room you must give both booklets to the Invigilator; if you do not, you may lose all the marks for this paper.

MARKS | DO NOT WRITE IN THIS MARGIN

Total marks — 20

You are preparing an application for the job advertised below and you write an e-mail in **German** to the company.

Hotel Seepark
GERHART-HAUPTMANN-STRAßE — 79110 FREIBURG

Wir suchen für unser Seepark Hotel ab sofort **einen Rezeptionist/eine Rezeptionistin.**

Ihr Profil:

Sie haben

- sehr gute Deutsch- und Englischkenntnisse
- Berufserfahrung in vergleichbarer Position/an der Rezeption

Sie sind

- organisiert, freundlich und stressresistent
- flexibel und zuverlässig

Für weiter Information können Sie uns unter info@hotelseepark.de kontaktieren.

To help you to write your e-mail, you have been given the following checklist.

You must include **all** of these points:

- Personal details (name, age, where you live)
- School/college/education experience until now
- Skills/interests you have which make you right for the job
- Related work experience
- Your reason for wanting to work in Germany
- What you plan to do when you leave school/college

Use all of the above to help you write the e-mail in **German**. The e-mail should be approximately 120—150 words. You may use a German dictionary.

MARKS | DO NOT WRITE IN THIS MARGIN

ANSWER SPACE

[Turn over

ANSWER SPACE (continued)

MARKS DO NOT WRITE IN THIS MARGIN

ANSWER SPACE (continued)

ANSWER SPACE (continued)

[END OF QUESTION PAPER]

MARKS | DO NOT WRITE IN THIS MARGIN

ADDITIONAL SPACE FOR ANSWERS

ADDITIONAL SPACE FOR ANSWERS

MARKS | DO NOT WRITE IN THIS MARGIN

N5

National
Qualifications
2017

Mark

X734/75/03

**German
Listening**

FRIDAY, 2 JUNE
2:50 PM – 3:20 PM (approx)

Fill in these boxes and read what is printed below.

Full name of centre

Town

Forename(s)

Surname

Number of seat

Date of birth
Day   Month   Year

Scottish candidate number

Total marks — 20

Attempt ALL questions.

You will hear two items in German. **Before you hear each item, you will have one minute to study the questions.** You will hear each item three times, with an interval of one minute between playings. You will then have time to answer the questions before hearing the next item.

You may NOT use a German dictionary.

Write your answers clearly, in **English**, in the spaces provided in this booklet. Additional space for answers is provided at the end of this booklet. If you use this space you must clearly identify the question number you are attempting.

Use **blue** or **black** ink.

You are not allowed to leave the examination room until the end of the test.

Before leaving the examination room you must give this booklet to the Invigilator; if you do not, you may lose all the marks for this paper.

✕SQA
©

MARKS | DO NOT WRITE IN THIS MARGIN

Total marks — 20

Attempt ALL questions

Item 1

Max talks about where he lives.

(a) Where does Max live? Tick (✓) the correct box.   1

	Tick (✓)
In the city centre.	
On a farm.	
In a village.	

(b) Why is his home important to him?   1

_____

_____

(c) What does Max say about where he lives? State any **two** things.   2

_____

_____

(d) Max says there are disadvantages of where he lives. What problems does he mention? State **two** things.   2

_____

_____

(e) Why is Max unhappy about asking his parents to take him places by car? State **one** thing.   1

_____

(f) Max meets his friends in the town at the weekend. What do they do? State **two** things.   1

_____

_____

MARKS

Item 2

Hannah and Max discuss the advantages and disadvantages of life in the town and in the country.

(a) How long has Hannah lived in Munich?

1

_____

(b) Where exactly did Hannah live before she moved to Munich?

1

_____

_____

(c) What did Hannah used to do in her free time? State any **two** things.

2

_____

_____

(d) What does Hannah miss about her old life? State any **two** things.

2

_____

_____

(e) What disadvantages of life in the country does she mention? State any **one** thing.

1

_____

_____

(f) Why does Hannah like living in Munich? State any **two** things.

2

_____

_____

(g) What benefit did Munich have for her mother?

1

_____

_____

[Turn over

MARKS | DO NOT WRITE IN THIS MARGIN

Item 2 (continued)

(h) Complete the sentence.   **2**

Hannah wants to live _____ when she is older because

there are more _____.

[END OF QUESTION PAPER]

MARKS DO NOT WRITE IN THIS MARGIN

ADDITIONAL SPACE FOR ANSWERS

Page five

MARKS | DO NOT WRITE IN THIS MARGIN

ADDITIONAL SPACE FOR ANSWERS

National Qualifications 2017

X734/75/13

German
Listening Transcript

FRIDAY, 2 JUNE

2:50 PM — 3:20 PM (approx)

This paper must not be seen by any candidate.

The material overleaf is provided for use in an emergency only (eg the recording or equipment proving faulty) or where permission has been given in advance by SQA for the material to be read to candidates with additional support needs. The material must be read exactly as printed.

Instructions to reader(s):

For each item, read the English **once**, then read the German **three times**, with an interval of 1 minute between the three readings. On completion of the third reading, pause for the length of time indicated in brackets after the item, to allow the candidates to write their answers.

Where special arrangements have been agreed in advance to allow the reading of the material, those sections marked **(f)** should be read by a female speaker and those marked **(m)** by a male; those sections marked **(t)** should be read by the teacher.

(t)   Item Number One

Max talks about where he lives.

You now have one minute to study the questions for Item Number One.

(m) Ich wohne auf einem Bauernhof in der Nähe von Heidelberg. Unser Bauernhof ist ein Weingut auf dem wir viele Trauben und auch Gemüse haben.

Es ist mir sehr wichtig, hier zu wohnen und zu arbeiten, denn mein Vater und mein Großvater haben auch hier gewohnt und gearbeitet.

Auf dem Bauernhof ist es sehr ruhig und sauber. Es ist wirklich wunderschön und wir haben eine tolle Aussicht auf den Fluss.

Trotzdem gibt es Nachteile. Das Problem ist, es kann abends einsam sein, weil meine Freunde alle weit weg wohnen. Ich sehe meine Freunde in der Schule, aber auf dem Land sind die Verkehrsverbindungen schlecht. Ich muss immer meine Eltern fragen, ob sie mich mit dem Auto fahren können. Das gefällt mir nicht, weil ich selbstständig sein möchte.

Aber am Wochenende gehe ich oft mit meinen Freunden in die Stadt. Wir gehen gerne ins Kino oder in den Jugendklub. Die Stadt hat viele Unterhaltungsmöglichkeiten für Jugendliche, aber ich kann mir nicht vorstellen, in der Stadt zu wohnen. Dort ist es mir zu laut und es gibt zu viele Leute. Obwohl es Nachteile gibt, liebe ich das Leben auf dem Bauernhof.

(2 minutes)

(t) Item Number Two

Hannah and Max discuss the advantages and disadvantages of life in the town and in the country.

You now have one minute to study the questions for Item Number Two.

(m) Seit wann wohnst du in München, Hannah?

(f) Ich wohne seit drei Jahren hier.

(m) Und wo hast du früher gewohnt?

(f) Früher habe ich in einem Dorf an der Grenze zu Österreich gewohnt. Dort war ich bei meinem Vater, weil meine Eltern nicht mehr zusammen waren. Aber mein Vater hat wieder geheiratet und ich mag meine Stiefmutter nicht, deswegen lebe ich jetzt gemeinsam mit meiner Mutter in München.

(m) Wie war das Leben in einem kleinen Dorf?

(f) Ich war jung und es war ganz okay. Es gab einige kleine Geschäfte und ein Eiscafé, aber nichts Besonderes. Ich hatte ein paar Freunde im Dorf und wir hatten Spaß.

(m) Was hast du in deiner Freizeit gemacht?

(f) Ich habe meine Freunde besucht und wir haben zusammen Sport getrieben, ferngesehen und geplaudert. Manchmal gab es im Sommer Grillpartys bei Freunden. Wir haben viel gelacht und danach im Freien gezeltet.

(m) Vermisst du das Leben auf dem Land?

(f) Ja. Ich vermisse meine Freunde und auch die frische Luft. Es ist sicherer auf dem Land und das Leben ist nicht so hektisch.

(m) Gibt es deiner Meinung nach auch Nachteile, wenn man auf dem Land wohnt?

(f) Klar gibt es Nachteile. Es gibt keine Busse und es ist nicht viel los für junge Leute.

(m) Wie findest du dein Leben hier in einer Großstadt?

(f) Ich mag München. Es hat alles, was man braucht und es ist nie langweilig. Ich kann zum Beispiel oft ins Kino gehen und es gibt große Einkaufszentren, wo man gut einkaufen kann. Meine Mutter hat ziemlich schnell eine Arbeit in München gefunden, und auf dem Land ist das nicht so einfach.

(m) Und wo willst du später wohnen?

(f) Bestimmt in einer großen Stadt, da es mehr Freizeitmöglichkeiten gibt.

(2 minutes)

(t) End of test.

Now look over your answers.

[END OF TRANSCRIPT]

[BLANK PAGE]

DO NOT WRITE ON THIS PAGE

NATIONAL 5

Answers

NATIONAL 5 GERMAN 2015

Reading

Text 1

(a) *Accept any one of:* Shiver/quiver/tremble/shake/quake

(b) • Do not sit (at a desk) <u>for hours</u>

• (Take) a break/pause <u>every 90 minutes/every hour and a half/after 90 minutes</u>

(c) *Any one from:*

• Her <u>hands</u> sweat/she has sweaty <u>hands</u>

• She loses her appetite/has no appetite/can't eat

(d) (i) (She practises/works on/does/goes over/prepares) it with a/her <u>friend</u>

NB: insist on **friend (singular)**

(ii) *Any one from:*

• They do it in a new environment/surroundings/place

• in a café <u>in town/in the city</u>

• the <u>school</u> library

(e) • (Exam nerves are) normal/necessary

(one adjective is sufficient)

NB: Exam nerves are normal and necessary would only be awarded   **1 mark**

• Without fear/worry you wouldn't take it/them seriously/Without stress, your exams would not come first

NB: "Fear of exams is normal or you wouldn't take it seriously" should be awarded   **2 marks**

(f) (i) <u>Failing</u> (the exam) would be/is a <u>disaster/catastrophe</u>

(ii) *Any one from:*

• I (have) prepared/worked (for the exam)

• I hope/aim/plan to get (a) good grade(s)/mark(s)/result(s)/I will do well

NB: Insist on future intention

Text 2

(a) They paid <u>half</u> of her <u>travel/trip/journey</u> (costs)

(b) • Contact <u>between young people/teenagers in India and Germany</u>

• Tolerance between <u>the</u> (two) <u>countries/between India and Germany/both lands</u>

(c) As a sign/symbol/gesture of friendship/to show friendship/to mark her friendship

(d) *Any three from:*

• (Lots of) outings/trips/excursions

• <u>Every evening/night/in the evening</u> there was a celebration/party/festival

• There was Indian food <u>every evening/in the evening/for dinner</u>

• A visit/trip/went to the parliament building (in New Delhi)

NB: Every evening they had a party with Indian food would be awarded **2 marks**. They had a party with Indian food would get **0 marks** because there is no indication of regularity.

(e) • Two pupils showed her books which <u>they</u> (had) read <u>in German</u>

NB: It must be clear that the pupils read the books

• Three boys told her about <u>two weeks</u> they spent in <u>Hamburg/Germany</u> (with a church group) **OR** time spent in <u>Hamburg/Germany with a church group</u>

NB: It must be clear that the three boys spent time in Germany

(f) **BOX 2:** She wants to promote understanding between the two countries

Text 3

(a) **BOX 2:** Sara's work is not perfect but she is a good pupil

(b) *Any three from:*

• It was (great) <u>fun</u>

• It is creative <u>work</u>

• You can work with/use your hands

• You can experiment with/try out <u>new ideas</u>

(c) • It <u>tasted</u> great/it was tasty/yummy/tasteful

• They sold it/you could buy it in <u>the confectioner's/in the (cake) shop/bakery</u>

(d) • (Sitting/Passing/Doing well in) exams

• <u>Developing/discovering/finding</u> new talent(s) (one verb needed)

NB: Accept "new talents to discover/develop" despite awkward word order

(e) *Any two from:*

• It offers (an) insight(s) into/a view/experience of (the world of) work/You see/saw into/become familiar with (the world of) work

• You can <u>learn from/through</u> (your own) experience

• You can <u>make/get/gain</u> (personal) contact(s)

Writing

General Marking Principles

Candidates will write a piece of extended writing in the modern language by addressing six bullet points. These bullet points will follow on from a job-related scenario. The bullet points will cover the four contexts of society, learning, employability and culture to allow candidates to use and adapt learned material. The first four bullet points will be the same each year and the last two will change to suit the scenario. Candidates need to address these "unpredictable bullet points" in detail to access the full range of marks.

Category	Mark	Content	Accuracy	Language resource — variety, range, structures
Very good	20	The job advert has been addressed in a full and balanced way. The candidate uses detailed language. The candidate addresses the advert completely and competently, **including information in response to both unpredictable bullet points.** A range of verbs/verb forms, tenses and constructions is used. Overall this comes over as a competent, well thought-out and serious application for the job.	The candidate handles all aspects of grammar and spelling accurately, although the language may contain one or two minor errors. Where the candidate attempts to use language more appropriate to Higher, a slightly higher number of inaccuracies need not detract from the overall very good impression.	The candidate is comfortable with the first person of the verb and generally uses a different verb in each sentence. Some modal verbs and infinitives may be used. There is good use of adjectives, adverbs and prepositional phrases and, where appropriate, word order. There may be a range of tenses. The candidate uses co-ordinating conjunctions and/or subordinate clauses where appropriate. The language of the e-mail flows well.
Good	16	The job advert has been addressed competently. There is less evidence of detailed language. The candidate uses a reasonable range of verbs/verb forms. Overall, the candidate has produced a genuine, reasonably accurate attempt at applying for the specific job, **even though he/she may not address one of the unpredictable bullet points.**	The candidate handles a range of verbs fairly accurately. There are some errors in spelling, adjective endings and, where relevant, case endings. Use of accents is less secure, where appropriate. Where the candidate is attempting to use more complex vocabulary and structures, these may be less successful, although basic structures are used accurately. There may be one or two examples of inaccurate dictionary use, especially in the unpredictable bullet points.	There may be repetition of verbs. There may be examples of listing, in particular when referring to school/college experience, without further amplification. There may be one or two examples of a co-ordinating conjunction, but most sentences are simple sentences. The candidate keeps to more basic vocabulary, particularly in response to either or both unpredictable bullet points.

Category	Mark	Content	Accuracy	Language resource — variety, range, structures
Satisfactory	12	The job advert has been addressed fairly competently. The candidate makes limited use of detailed language. The language is fairly repetitive and uses a limited range of verbs and fixed phrases, e.g. *I like, I go, I play*. The candidate copes fairly well with areas of personal details, education, skills, interests and work experience but does not deal fully with the two unpredictable bullet points **and indeed may not address either or both of the unpredictable bullet points.** On balance however the candidate has produced a satisfactory job application in the specific language.	The verbs are generally correct, but may be repetitive. There are quite a few errors in other parts of speech — gender of nouns, cases, singular/plural confusion, for instance. Prepositions may be missing, e.g. *I go the town*. Overall, there is more correct than incorrect.	The candidate copes with the first and third person of a few verbs, where appropriate. A limited range of verbs is used. Sentences are basic and mainly brief. There is minimal use of adjectives, probably mainly after *is* e.g. *Chemistry is interesting*. The candidate has a weak knowledge of plurals. There may be several spelling errors, e.g. reversal of vowel combinations.
Unsatisfactory	8	The job advert has been addressed in an uneven manner and/or with insufficient use of detailed language. The language is repetitive, e.g. *I like, I go, I play* may feature several times. There may be little difference between Satisfactory and Unsatisfactory. **Either or both of the unpredictable bullet points may not have been addressed.** There may be one sentence which is not intelligible to a sympathetic native speaker.	Ability to form tenses is inconsistent. There are errors in many other parts of speech — gender of nouns, cases, singular/plural confusion, for instance. Several errors are serious, perhaps showing mother tongue interference. The detail in the unpredictable bullet points may be very weak. Overall, there is more incorrect than correct.	The candidate copes mainly only with the personal language required in bullet points 1 and 2. The verbs *is* and *study* may also be used correctly. Sentences are basic. An English word may appear in the writing. There may be an example of serious dictionary misuse.

Category	Mark	Content	Accuracy	Language resource — variety, range, structures
Poor	4	The candidate has had considerable difficulty in addressing the job advert. There is little evidence of the use of detailed language. Three or four sentences may not be understood by a sympathetic native speaker. **Either or both of the unpredictable bullet points may not have been addressed.**	Many of the verbs are incorrect. There are many errors in other parts of speech — personal pronouns, gender of nouns, cases, singular/plural confusion, prepositions, for instance. The language is probably inaccurate throughout the writing.	The candidate cannot cope with more than one or two basic verbs. The candidate displays almost no knowledge of the present tense of verbs. Verbs used more than once may be written differently on each occasion. Sentences are very short. The candidate has a very limited vocabulary. Several English words may appear in the writing. There are examples of serious dictionary misuse.
Very poor	0	The candidate is unable to address the job advert. **The two unpredictable bullet points may not have been addressed.** Very little is intelligible to a sympathetic native speaker.	Virtually nothing is correct.	The candidate may only cope with the verbs *to have* and *to be*. Very few words are written correctly in the modern language. English words are used. There may be several examples of mother tongue interference. There may be several examples of serious dictionary misuse.

Listening

Item 1

(a) 13th August

(b) Four years ago

OR

When he was 11 years old

(c) *Any two from:*

- (On) Wednesday(s)/every Wednesday
- Every second/other weekend
- Four weeks in the (school) holidays

(d) *Any two from:*

- (Spends) Christmas/it with his mother
- Visits/Sees/Stays with his dad two days later
- He gets two lots of/twice as many presents/presents from both parents

(e) He (always) gets good marks/grades/results

(f) **BOX 3:** He is positive

Item 2

(a) (Martin is Erik's) young(er)/little/small brother

(b) *Any one from:*

- They get on (quite) well

OR

- He has a good relationship with his brother/It is good
- He can get on his nerves/he sometimes/now and again gets on his nerves/gets on his nerves when he comes into his room without knocking
- He likes him

(c) • Mother: Secretary/Works in an office (in town)

NB: Secretary in a bureau is acceptable

- Father: Policeman/Police/Police officer

(d) His mum is allergic (to dogs)

NB: Any recognisable spelling of "allergic" acceptable

(e) (i) Piano

(ii) 3 years

(f) *Any three from:*

- He has three or four (really) good/close friends
- They are (quite) loud/noisy
- Fun/funny/a good laugh
- They have the same/similar interests

(g) *Any two from:*

- Go jogging in the (town) park
- Ride their bikes/go on bike rides/tours/cycle in the (local)area/neighbourhood
- Play in/for the school football team/Play football for the school
- Go to the cinema regularly
- Watch adventure films

NATIONAL 5 GERMAN 2016

Reading

Text 1

(a) Raw material(s)/commodities

(b) • Put (a) sticker(s)/sign(s)/message(s)/note(s) saying "No adverts"

OR

- Put (a) sticker(s)/sign(s)/message(s)/note(s) on the (house/front) door

(Candidate needs to mention either the message or where the message is to gain mark)

(c) • They come/are transported by air/plane/are flown in (to Germany) (ignore wrong tenses)

- This causes (air) pollution

(d) • It (often) looks better/nicer (insist on comparative)

- It is (usually) (much) cheaper/more reasonably priced/better value/more inexpensive/less expensive/not as expensive as a new one (insist on comparative)

(e) • (They can) exchange/swap clothes

- Share sports stuff/things/articles/gear/equipment

(f) (i) Try/attempt to repair/fix (broken) things/(a) bike(s)/(a) washing machine(s)

(ii) Electrical equipment/goods/electronics/appliance(s)

Text 2

(a) • Hardly any/not many/(a) few/almost no/very little

- **Tasteless/not tasty/doesn't taste nice/bad tasting (insist on suggestion of negative taste)**

(b) • The pupils/they do the cooking/cook/make their own food/lunch (themselves) (every day)

- Every two weeks another class is responsible for lunch

NB: A different class cooks every two weeks — 2 marks

NB: They cook for two weeks — 1 mark; lacks idea of rotation

(c) • The pupils no longer/don't heat up food/cook in the microwave/eat microwave food/use the microwave (when they go home)

- They (want to now) cook with/use fresh ingredients/they cook/eat fresh food/cook meals fresh

(d) • Accept/take (on) responsibility/be responsible

- Work together/with others/collaborate/cooperate/teamwork
- The cost of food/groceries/meals

(e) • The food is (now) tasty/tastier/delicious/yummy/nice(r)

- It/the food is now healthy/healthier/good for your health
- The pupils can get a free second helping/portion/two (meals) for the price of one   **(Any 2 from 3)**

Text 3

(a) • (You can) (always) do <u>what</u> you want/make your own decisions/choose what you want to do

• (You are) responsible for/in charge of (your own) <u>time</u> management/manage your (own) <u>time</u>

• (You can) <u>develop/spend time on/try out</u> your own ideas/make your <u>idea(s)</u> a reality **(Any 2 from 3)**

(b) (i) (At the) <u>Sunday market/market in town</u>

(NB: market + one piece of information necessary to gain point)

(ii) • <u>(Quite) a lot of/Many students</u> (have) bought his clothes/wear his clothes

• <u>He/I</u> began to see/saw his/my clothes/them <u>in/around/about town/in the street</u>

(c) • He had enough money for/bought/got/could afford a <u>used/second hand</u> car

• (Enough money for an) <u>eight-week</u> trip/journey/holiday through/to Italy

• He opened/got/had/started a (small) shop (in his home town) **(Any 2 from 3)**

(d) • (You need) insurance

• (You need to) repair/fix (a) <u>sewing</u> machine(s) **(Any 1 from 2)**

(e) They wanted to change/alter his jacket(s)/blazer(s) <u>and/or</u> shirt(s)

(f) **BOX 2:** It's worthwhile, although there are also difficulties
NB: no marks awarded for more than one tick

Writing

Please see the assessment criteria for Writing on pages 104–106.

Listening

Item 1

(a) • A <u>beach</u> house (on Corfu)

• A <u>holiday</u> flat/apartment (in Spain)

• A caravan (in the Alps) **(Any 2 from 3)**

(b) • (You can) live/stay/spend time/be <u>together</u>

• (You can) <u>share</u> the work/<u>share</u> cooking/<u>share</u> washing up/(You can) <u>all</u> work/<u>all</u> cook/<u>all</u> wash up

• It's cheap<u>er</u> (than a hotel)

• (Maybe) your friends might speak another language **(Any 1 from 4)**

(c) In (the) <u>south</u> (of) France (in a villa)

(d) In a (holiday) brochure/leaflet/pamphlet

(e) • Lying/relaxing/spending time <u>in the sun</u>/<u>sun</u>bathing

• Swimming <u>in the sea</u>

• Going to the (large) <u>shopping mall/centre(s)</u> (in the next town) **(Any 2 from 3)**

(f) **BOX 2:** She's tried it and won't do it again

NB: no marks awarded for more than one tick

Item 2

(a) His boss/manager

(b) • Holidays <u>abroad</u> are not for her/she does not like holidays <u>abroad</u>

• You can have a <u>good</u> holiday/time (in Germany)

• You can go (everywhere) by car/Drive around

• You can get to know the country/place/countryside/area/land (better) **(Any 2 from 4)**

(c) • (To forget) stress/a hectic life/It's stressful/hectic (in the town)

• Peace/quiet is (very) important to him **(Any 1 from 2)**

(d) The <u>North Sea</u>/On the <u>north coast</u> (in a holiday home)

(e) The weather is/was bad/It rained (last year)(when he was there)/It rains (all the time)/wet

(f) • It's a compromise

• It's not (too) far away

• It's not (too) expensive/it's (very) cheap **(Any 2 from 3)**

(g) • She was/went/stayed/lived there (already) <u>with her sister</u>/<u>two years ago</u>

NB: disregard "for two years"; it must be clear that event is in the past

• She wants (to experience/see) something new **(Any 1 from 2)**

(h) • (It's good for) shopping/(Good) shopping facilities/opportunities/The shops

• At home/At their (own) house/They are not going away

(j) Tidy/clean/clear out/sort out/organise the <u>garage</u>

NATIONAL 5 GERMAN 2017

Reading

Text 1

(a) The best feeling <u>in the world</u>

(b) • She was born with <u>no arms</u>/first person <u>without arms</u> to become a pilot
   • She steers/pilots/controls/flies the plane with her foot/feet
   • She did it against all expectations/(the) odds/she exceeded expectations   **(Any 2 from 3)**

(c) • They were worried/troubled/concerned/had concerns
   • They had reservations/doubts/were hesitant
   • They supported her (to overcome challenges)/they were supportive   **(Any 2 from 3)**

(d) • Climbing <u>with her friend(s)</u>/climbing <u>every week</u>
   • (Goes to/is a member/part of a) <u>sailing/yacht(ing)</u> (club/team) (for many years)
   • Spends <u>every second weekend/every two weekends/</u> by the <u>sea</u>/at the <u>seaside</u>/on the <u>beach</u> (ignore preposition eg on/at sea)   **(Any 2 from 3)**

(e) • (Many) <u>interviews/interviewed on TV</u>
   • Spoke at (her old) school(s) about her <u>adventure(s)</u>
   • Organised (free) flights for <u>disabled children</u>   **(Any 2 from 3)**

(f) • Don't/never give up (on your dreams)
   • Live/follow/fulfil your dream/don't dream your life/make your dream a reality   **(Any 1 from 2)**

Text 2

(a) In the <u>neighbouring</u> woods/forest/woods <u>nearby</u>/<u>next</u> to school

(b) • Pupils <u>get to know</u> the (local) area/surroundings/ environment (better)
   • Pupils <u>get to know</u> nature (better)
   • They use their (all) <u>senses</u> (to learn)
   • They learn about (the) <u>natural habitat</u>(s)/<u>biosphere</u> (of insects, plants and animals)/the teacher teaches about <u>insects, plants and animals</u>

   OR

   • They learn about <u>insects, plants and animals</u>
   • It is an <u>important</u> <u>experience</u> (for all children)   **(Any 2 from 5)**

(c) • He hates being indoors/sitting in the class when the sun is shining/when it's sunny/he likes being outside in the sunshine/he enjoys being in the sun/he likes the sun/you get to be in the sun
   • (He gets to) work (together) with his friend(s)
   • They solve/do <u>(a) puzzle(s)/riddle(s)/problem(s)</u> (together)
   • They <u>play</u> (games) (together)
   • <u>Fun</u> to learn about animals   **(Any 2 from 5)**

(d) • The <u>petals</u> of the <u>flowers/blossom</u>
   • The <u>veins</u> of (a) <u>leaf/leaves</u>
   • The <u>bark/crust</u> of (a) <u>tree(s)</u>   **(Any 2 from 3)**

(e) • They <u>spend time</u> in the fresh air/<u>get/gives them</u> fresh air
   • They exercise/move <u>regularly</u>
   • The immune system/<u>becomes stronger/strengthen</u>/ a <u>strong(er)</u> immune system
   • Increase(d) (in) oxygen (levels)
   • They concentrate <u>better/more</u>   **(Any 2 from 5)**

(f) Not (always) reliable/unreliable

Text 3

(a) (Almost) a third

(b) • To do something/it is unusual/different
   • To do something/it is rewarding/worthwhile
   • To gain/get/have/collect (some) work experience
   • To travel/see/explore <u>the world</u>
   • To discover/experience/see/learn about/find (a) new country/countries/land(s) <u>and</u> culture(s)   **(Any 2 from 5)**

(c) (New) challenge(s)/demand(s)

(d) • They are (more) focussed
   • They have (useful) <u>life</u> experience/it is a <u>worthwhile/valuable</u> experience
   • They develop/strengthens (their) (a strong(er)) character/ they have a strong(er) character/ personality   **(Any 2 from 3)**

(e) <u>Interesting</u> CV(s)/résumé(s)/application(s)

(f) • (When you showed) initiative/shows
   • (When you) (can) <u>work</u>(ed)/<u>cope(d)</u> under pressure
   • When you <u>worked</u> in a team/team <u>work</u>/team <u>player</u>
   • (When you took on) responsibility/you are responsible (ignore tense)   **(Any 3 from 4)**

Writing

Please see the assessment criteria for Writing on pages 104–106.

Listening

Item 1

(a) On a farm

(b) • It's a vineyard/grow (their own) grapes/vegetables
   • Because his father <u>and</u> grandfather lived/worked here too/it/the farm belongs in his <u>family</u>/ it's a <u>family</u> business/it's been passed down for <u>generations</u>

(c) • They grow (their own) grapes/vegetables (do not accept if answer to part (b))
   • Peaceful/quiet
   • Clean
   • (Very) beautiful/pretty
   • (Great) <u>view</u> of the river/you can <u>see</u> the <u>river</u>
   • His friends live far away/friends don't live nearby

- Because his father and grandfather lived/worked here too/it/the farm belongs in his family/ it's a family business/it's been passed down for generations (do not accept if answer to part (b)) **(Any 2 from 7)**

(d) • It can be lonely (in the evenings)

- His friends live <u>far away</u>/friends don't live <u>nearby</u> (do not accept if answer to part (c))

- The <u>public</u> transport is bad/lack of/no <u>public</u> transport/there are few/no travel <u>connections</u> **(Any 2 from 3)**

(e) He wants to be independent/self-sufficient/to do his own thing/to go on his own/self-reliant/doesn't want to rely on parents

(f) Cinema <u>and</u> youth club/centre/club for young people/ person(s)

Item 2

(a) Three <u>years</u>

(b) • (In a village) on the Austrian <u>border</u>/<u>near</u> Austria

- With (her) dad (and stepmum) **(Any 1 from 2)**

(c) • <u>Visited/saw/met/had fun with/went out with</u> friend(s)

- Did/goes to sport (together)

- Watched <u>TV</u>

- Chatted

- Went to (a) BBQ(s)

- Laughed (lots)

- Went camping

- Went to shops/ice-cream parlour/cafe **(Any 2 from 8)**

(d) • Her friend(s)

- The fresh <u>air</u>

- The security/it is safe(r)

- Slower pace of life/it is not so hectic (in the country)/more hectic/stressful <u>in the town</u> **(Any 2 from 4)**

(e) • There is/are <u>no</u> bus(es)/can't take/get a bus

- There is not much happening <u>for young people</u>/ there's not a lot/nothing <u>for young people</u> (to do) **(Any 1 from 2)**

(f) • It has everything you need

- It is <u>never/not</u> boring

- (You can go to the) cinema

- There are (big) shopping <u>centre</u>(s)/<u>good</u> (for) shopping/<u>good</u> shops **(Any 2 from 4)**

(g) She got a job there (quickly)/more job opportunities (than in the county)/could find a job/found work (quickly)/<u>more</u> jobs/it was hard(er) to get a job in the country

(h) • In the city/(big)town

- Free time <u>opportunities</u> (there)/(things) to do

Acknowledgements

Permission has been sought from all relevant copyright holders and Hodder Gibson is grateful for the use of the following:

Image © wavebreakmedia/Shutterstock.com (2015 Reading page 2);
Image © OLJ Studio/Shutterstock.com (2015 Reading page 4);
Image © Pressmaster/Shutterstock.com (2015 Reading page 6);
Image © patpat/Shutterstock.com (2016 Reading page 2);
Image © Guy Shapira/Shutterstock.com (2016 Reading page 4);
Image © wavebreakmedia/Shutterstock.com (2016 Reading page 6);
Image © michaeljung/Shutterstock.com (2017 Reading page 2);
Image © Hurst Photo/Shutterstock.com (2017 Reading page 4);
Image © Halfpoint/Shutterstock.com (2017 Reading page 6).